DEAL & WALMER

A Celebration

Tom Burnham

Gregory Holyoake

DEAL & WALMER
A Celebration

Watercolours   TOM BURNHAM

Commentary   GREGORY HOLYOAKE

DEAL CASTLE & BEACH BOATS

T. Burnham '02

for
MARLENE,
BEN & JACK

First published in an edition limited to 1250 copies
in 2009 by The Dovecote Press Ltd
Stanbridge, Wimborne Minster, Dorset BH21 4JD

ISBN 978-1-904-34974-7

Text © Gregory Holyoake 2009
Paintings © Tom Burnham 2009

Designed by David Burnett
Photography by Ian Giles

Gregory Holyoake and Tom Burnham have asserted their
rights under the Copyright, Designs and Patent Act 1988
to be identified as authors of this work

Typeset in Sabon
Printed and bound in Singapore by KHL Printing Co. Pte Ltd
All the papers used by The Dovecote Press are natural, recyclable products
made from wood grown in sustainable, well-managed forests

A CIP catalogue record for this book is available
from the British Library

1 3 5 7 9 8 6 4 2

CONTENTS

Deal was originally a limb of Sandwich, regarded as the premier Cinque Port. When Sandwich Haven silted up in Tudor times, Deal rose to prosperity by serving shipping in the Downs Anchorage.

In 1699, Deal was granted its Charter of Incorporation as a 'borough and market town' by William III. At first, the Mayor and Corporation held their council meetings in a house rented from a widow, Anna Lawrence, in Lower Street (now High Street).

In 1702, it was decided to build a Court Hall, Gaol and Bridewell (or 'house of correction'). This noble building stood between Market Street and King Street. It was surmounted by a cupola containing a 'fire and market bell'. Cobbles from the pavement mark the site of the old fish market in Market Street.

An early mayor was the fiery Thomas Powell, whose religious fervour earned him national notoriety in the reign of Queen Anne. He was praised profusely by Daniel Defore for his indefatigable endeavours to rescue stricken sailors during the Great Storm of 1703.

In 1803, the present Town Hall was built. It is an imposing structure with a central triangular pediment over a Venetian window. A row of stout Tuscan columns guard the forecourt where formerly the town's fire engine was stored. At the rear were four cramped cells, since Deal was originally policed by a Town Sergeant assisted by twelve parish constables.

The Council Chamber remains a most dignified room. It is graced with paintings of dignitaries connected with the town and port. There are portraits of King William III, Sir Winston Churchill and Queen Elizabeth the Queen Mother as Lord Warden of the Cinque Ports. Most prominent is the 'blue stocking' author, Mrs. Elizabeth Carter, posing in a borrowed gown reading in a garden, painted by Joseph Highmore (circa 1738).

The Mayor's Parlour is a gem. Pride of place hangs a watercolour by J.M.W Turner: 'Deal In A Storm' (circa 1820) The artist achieves his dramatic effect by subtle pastel shades. It is the only Turner painting to feature a stroke of lightning.

In 1457, the Mayor of Sandwich, John Drury, was killed in a French raid. Thereafter, successive Mayors have worn black robes denoting mourning (Cinque Port Mayors generally wear scarlet). Deal's Mayor, in sympathy, wears half mourning with a black robe and black bows tied to his gold chain of office.

It is a further peculiarity that whenever Deal's Mayor boards a Royal Navy ship in the Downs he automatically assumes the rank of Admiral.

St. Leonard's Church

St. Leonard's Church has served the parish for 800 years at Upper Deal. Built over a mile from the seashore, its original purpose was to minister to the needs of this humble farming community. Later, it began to accommodate seamen and sailors when the Navy Yard opened in Stuart times.

St. Leonard's dates from circa 1180 and was built on a high mound where four roads now meet. Today, it presents a confusing mixture of architectural styles: a 12th century nave, a 13th century chancel, a 17th century tower and a 19th century porch with annexe.

The red brick tower, which is surmounted by a white timber lantern with a cupola, dates from 1686. It appears on early charts of the Downs as an important landmark for shipping and for that reason it was maintained by Trinity House. Symonson's Map of Kent depicts it with a steeple but this crashed through the roof causing immense damage.

First rector was Richard de la Wyche (1197-1253) better known as St. Richard of Chichester. St. Richard is remembered for his prayer: 'May I see Thee more clearly, love Thee more dearly and follow Thee more nearly, day by day'. A modern church built for the mining community is dedicated to this unwordly medieval priest.

St. Leonard's contains three fascinating memorial brasses. Thomas Boys is depicted as a knight in full armour kneeling at prayer. He was a gentleman-at-arms who attended Henry VIII at the Siege of Boulogne in 1544. For his loyal service he was rewarded by being appointed Mayor of Calais and Captain of Deal Castle.

A second brass commemorates Thomas Baker, earliest known Deputy who acted in the absence of the Mayor of Sandwich until Deal received its charter. The third brass is most unusual for it is a 'chrism' brass showing the infant daughter, wrapped in swaddling clothes, of the sorrowful parson, Thomas Consant.

One great treasure is the modest west gallery constructed for the exclusive use of the pilots of Deal. A central painting presents a magnificent man-o'-war, fully rigged and under sail. This recalls the Great Storm of 1703 when four warships founded on the Goodwins and 1,100 sailors drowned in a single night. Deftly, the artist has included both the bow and stern of the vessel.

Joshua Coppin, first Mayor of Deal, is interred in the nave. He lived at the nearby Manor House, from the rooftop of which smugglers are said to have signalled secretly to ships arriving in the Downs.

Another tomb is that of Vice-Admiral Sir Francis Samuel Drake (died 1789), a respectable descendant of Sir Francis Drake, the Elizabethan sea rover. A host of brave mariners are buried in this raised churchyard and their headstones include chiseled images of skulls and crossbones, anchors and hour glasses.

Deal Castle is the largest of the three castles – Walmer, Deal and Sandown – built by Henry VIII 'to keep the Downs'. After Henry's quarrel with the Pope over his intended divorce of Catherine of Aragon and his assumption of Head of the Church in England, he feared invasion from Catholic France and Spain. He therefore proceeded to strengthen the Kent coastline between 1539-40.

It has little been noticed that the castles' construction coincided with the controversial publication of Henry's 'Great Bible' in English.

These revolutionary fortifications, built for the age of gunpowder, represent the final stage of castle architecture. Accidentally reflecting the shape of the Tudor rose, their design consists of a round keep surrounded by a double circle of 'petals' or bastions. Deal – 'The Greate Castle' – is 'sex-foil' while Walmer and Sandown are both 'quatre-foil' in style. Low, squat and concealed from enemy shipping their circular construction not only deflected enemy cannon balls but provided a 360 degrees field of gunfire.

Traditional features were maintained by the architect, Stephan von Haschenperg – a central well, a dry moat, a drawbridge on the landward side and a gatehouse protected by a stout studded door, five 'murder holes' and a portcullis. Their rapid construction – 18 months – was interrupted by the earliest strike on record when workmen downed tools and demanded a pay rise from 5d to 6d per day.

Eventually, 'great gunnys' at Deal Castle comprised one cannon, three culverins, four demi-culverins, five sacres, two minions and one falcon. The brass cannon's bore was 7 inches and its extreme range was over three miles while the lesser guns, such as the falcon, carried smaller shot further but did less damage. At first there was a delay in firing this new armament for want of an 'Inginier'.

Deal Castle was so far advanced by the winter of 1539 that it welcomed a royal visitor. Henry's fourth prospective wife, Anne of Cleves, crossed over from Calais attended by a colourful flotilla shortly after Christmas. It was her first glimpse of the sea and first journey in a ship. After landing at Deal, Anne 'taried there a certeine space in a castell newlie built' before proceeding towards London. Henry, excited at the prospect of a nubile young bride, rode out to greet her in disguise at Rochester. Alas, he dismissed Anne upon sight as 'a Flanders' mare'.

Elizabeth I inspected the castles during her royal progress across Kent in 1573. After leaving Dover, Good Queen Bess travelled through Walmer and Deal before being carried on a litter along the Ancient Highway to Sandwich. Ironically, none of the three Henrican castles saw hot fighting until the English Civil War when they passed repeatedly between Cavalier and Roundhead hands. Last time Deal Castle was fiercely defended was during the Second World War. A direct hit by a bomb demolished the hideous Governor's lodgings constructed in 1802. It was the opinion of inhabitants at that time that, unintentionally, Hitler had done the town a favour!

Middle Street forms the centre of a trio of historic streets in Deal, which together make up Kent's first Conservation Area. Beach Street follows the foreshore, High Street (formerly 'Lower Street') remains the commercial hub while Middle Street linked the Tudor castles. All three are lined with desirable Georgian and Victorian dwellings frequently snapped up and restored by Londoners who refer to this quaint quarter as 'Little Chelsea'.

Middle Street is redolent of the time when Deal was a thriving port. Shops, inns and warehouses jostle with redundant soup kitchens, slaughter houses and boatbuilders' yards. A private house on the corner of Brewer Street was once the Paragon Music Hall which had a dubious reputation. Patrons clamoured into the circle or stalls, boxes and bars for a raucous evening's entertainment. Grander homes – Vane House and Queen Anne House – testify, however, to the town's former prosperity.

Domestic dwellings retain their individual features. Different styles of doorways and dormers, footscrapers and fanlights, chimneys and shutters are a constant delight. Rooftops display an array of Dutch gables. Indeed, the curvilinear type is known architecturally as the 'Deal Gable'. There is a wonderful concentration of graceful gables at 'Dutch Corner'.

Myriad streets meander towards the seafront. All bear intriguing names. Many streets are named after prominent inns. The Hoop and Griffin in Griffin Street rivalled The Royal Hotel for seafaring patrons while The Royal Exchange atop Exchange Street offered them 'a full prospect of the Downs'. The Horse and Farrier alehouse stood in Farrier Street and The Royal Oak in Oak Street was the scene of lively concerts, banquets and balls.

Two adjoining streets commemorate civic dignitaries. Coppin Street is named after Joshua Coppin, Deal's first Mayor, while Brewer Street recalls John Brewer, Deal's first Recorder. Dolphin Street refers, not to the mammal, but to the mooring pole to which small craft were secured instead of drawing them up the shingle. Picturesque Portobello Court owes its exotic name to a sea captain who served with Admiral Vernon's modest fleet which courageously captured Portobello, in Panama, in 1739.

The names Golden and Silver Street, it is fancifully suggested, allude to the wealth acquired by the activities of smugglers. Romantic tales are told of smuggling but in reality this was a violent occupation. Middle Street was the scene of a pitched battle between the smugglers and the Revenue Men. Secret rooms, cunning hides and one rooftop run extending the length of Coppin Street are evidence of the extent of the 'Wicked Trade'. Little wonder the Georgian diarist, Fanny Burney, described Deal as a 'sad smuggling town'.

The King's Head (circa 1720) which nowadays gives a warm welcome to visitors was once a centre for smuggling. In 1776, the landlord, defiantly, took down his inn sign to avoid billeting dragoons sent by the government to combat this 'Wicked Trade'.

Undeniably, Deal's prosperity owed much to smuggling in times past. The port's proximity to the Continent, coupled with its long, lonely beach where small boats might glide on moonless nights undetected by the Revenue Men, was all that a smuggler might ask. Once landed, prohibited goods were speedily removed along the confusing maze of narrow streets to remote taverns – Jolly Sailor and Noah's Ark – for swift conveyance by pack horses to London.

Heyday of smuggling was the period from the mid 17th century to the early 19th century when Britain's expansion of world trade coincided with the necessity to finance wars in Europe and America.

At first, only luxury goods – tea, tobacco, spirits and fabric – were subject to duty but during the reign of George III (depicted on the inn sign) over 800 items became taxable. Contraband followed fashion. Ladies were tempted to buy cheap accessories – ribbons, lace, shoes, shawls, bead purses, silk slippers, kid gloves and ostrich plumes – openly from local boatmen.

Gentlefolk travelled down in their carriages to purchase rich materials – silk, satin, velvet and brocade – directly from Deal foreshore and these were turned into sumptuous gowns to be proudly worn at the London salons.

Smuggling became romanticised although, in truth, confrontations between smugglers and the authorities were bloody and brutal. A tombstone in St. George's churchyard commemorates Private John Elbeck who was shot at point blank range and fatally wounded by a midnight marauder.

Almost everyone was involved in this illicit trade from the boatmen, who were the actual carriers, to the magistrates who financed their nocturnal expeditions. Boats were customised for smuggling. Stout 'luggers' were fitted out with false masts and keels while sleek 'galleys' were adapted for speed to ensure a swift crossing to France. Artfully, they were painted white to merge with the surf to avoid pursuit by Revenue Men.

One trick was for the burly boatmen, on a return trip laden with contraband, was to carry their galley across the Goodwins at low tide and then row leisurely across the Downs. Revenue Men, in their cumbersome cutters, were compelled to give up the chase since they would be forced into sailing a tortuous route round the Sands.

Galleys with four or more oars were declared illegal since they could serve no other purpose than smuggling. If caught with `run` goods, their owners would be made to saw them in half although crafty boatmen then turned them into unique beach huts or homes.

St. George's Church

St. George's Church, intended as the 'chapel-of-ease' to St. Leonard's, is a handsome Queen Anne edifice that graces Deal's High Street. The Admiralty approved the building of this additional church since the main beneficiaries would be their own sailors when stationed in the Downs.

Land was purchased on former brewery property and building work commenced on this prime site in the summer of 1707. Champion of the cause was Admiral Sir Cloudesley Shovel whose fleet was frequently anchored offshore. Alas, this fine fighting seaman was shipwrecked because of imprecise navigation off the Scilly Isles that winter. Interest in this laudable project subsequently waned. For the next ten years all four walls were left open to the sky . . .

Eventually, an Act of Parliament authorised a tax to be levied upon coal entering the Port of Deal. Sufficient funds were thereby obtained for the completion of the building.

The new church dedicated to St. George-the-Martyr was consecrated on 16 June 1716. An early incumbent was the irascible Dr. Nicholas Carter, father of the blue stocking, Elizabeth, who served as Perpetual Curate for an incredible 56 years.

First Vicar, appointed when St. George's was elevated to a parish church in 1852, was the Rev. Henry Honywood D'Ombrain. His passion for roses culminated in the founding of both The Royal Horticultural Rose Society and The Society. Two species which D'Ombrain introduced into this country – 'Marechal Niel' and 'Bourbon' – are depicted on the sign of the adjacent Rose Hotel.

Naturally, since St. George's was intended as a 'Sailors' Church', there are numerous maritime architectural features. The topmost gallery was created exclusively for the boatmen who might suddenly leave as the wind changed mid service. The clattering of their heavy boots as they left by their own staircase would not disturb the congregation.

Perhaps, the most striking feature is the stained glass panorama of the foreshore in the lowest panel of the East Window. Landmarks depicted include Deal Castle, Prince of Wales Terrace and the Timeball Tower. Walmer lifeboat is also shown returning ashore after a rescue.

The churchyard contains the tombs of countless brave folk – pilots, pursers, captains, coastguards, officers of the East India Company and the Navy Yard – whose livelihoods depended upon the sea. By the south door is the grave of Commander David Ross, R.N., (died 1836) who was a personal friend of William IV. A large Celtic stone cross commemorates the fallen of the First World War. Sadly, the roll of honour includes the names of the two brilliant sons of the scholarly cleric, Rev St. Clair Tisdall.

Carter House

Carter House was the home of Deal's most famous resident, Elizabeth Carter (1717-1806) 'Mrs' Carter was a celebrated poet, author and translator who became a prominent member of the 'Bluestockings', an exclusive literary society in Georgian London.

Elizabeth's scholarship won her world renown. It elicted praise from Dr. Samuel Johnson who admired both her learning and her domesticity. She won from him this accolade: 'My old friend, Mrs Carter, could make a pudding as well as translate Epictetus and work a handkerchief as well as compose a poem.'

Elizabeth was the daughter of Rev. Nicolas Carter, the intolerant incumbent of St. George's Church. In the absence of a Vicarage, Nicolas and his young family lived in a property in Park Street which was so cramped they called it the 'Vinegar Bottle'.

During one of her visits to London Elizabeth was challenged to translate the works of a first century B.C. Greek philospher, Epictetus. This project took ten years to complete but when *The Life and Works of Epictetus* was published by subscription in 1758 it brought her instant fame and fortune.

Royalties from the first edition amounted to a phenomenal £1,000 and enabled her to purchase four adjoining seaside tenements in 1762. Elizabeth converted them into a single dwelling where she was visited by royalty and gentry who were all keen to win the friendship of Parson Carter's daughter.

Elizabeth's voluminous correspondence reveal the hustle and bustle of daily life in the port during the 18th century. She mentions the threat of invasion by the French, conflicts with the press gangs and the nocturnal activities of the smugglers. 'I hear nothing here but tea and brandy, and prohibitive clothing,' she lamented, 'which is bought up with a scandalous degree of eagerness by people of fashion and fortune.' (1772)

Her letters also reveal the great pride she took in her garden ablaze with roses, myrtles, geraniums and honeysuckles. In her sunny courtyard she planted an acorn which grew into a noble oak. Sadly, ivy sapped the life of this tree, claimed to be 'the most easterly in England'.

When Elizabeth contracted a painful illness known as 'St. Anthony's Fire' (ergotism) she bravely travelled alone to say farewell to her friends in London. She died in February 1806 and was interred in the grounds of Grosvenor Chapel, although all traces of her tomb have now vanished.

The Royal Hotel (circa 1720) is the only remaining building on our once crowded foreshore. Originally called The Three Kings, it changed its name after a visit from Princess Adelaide who arrived in the port to marry the Duke of Clarence, later William IV, 'The Sailor King', in July 1818.

This shy German bride never forgot the warm welcome she received from the townsfolk. As Queen Adelaide she became a generous benefactor and subscribed to the building of St. Andrew's, the boatmen's church, and the Royal Adelaide Baths, which stood just northwards of the hotel.

In the summer of 1801, Vice Admiral Lord Nelson was commanded by the Admiralty to check the vast invasion fleet that Napoleon Bonaparte was assembling off the French coast with which to invade England. Wracked with toothache, suffering from headcolds and constantly seasick, Nelson chose the Royal Hotel as his shore base although he returned each night to his flagship, *Medusa*, in the Downs.

The midnight commando raid which Nelson subsequently organised was a total disaster. His plan was to secretly tow the enemy ships away from their moorings and then either sink them or set them alight. In the event the expedition went horribly wrong – Napoleon had chained all his ships together – and many of Nelson's gallant seamen were killed or injured.

Among the casualties was his close companion, Captain Edward Thornbridge Parker, who subsequently died of his wounds and lies buried in St. George's churchyard. The Battle of Boulogne was Nelson's only defeat.

Nelson's mistress, Emma, and her accommodating husband, Sir William Hamilton, arrived in Deal to comfort the injured sailors. They hired a suite of rooms above the boathouse and made the occasion of their visit a brief summer holiday. Whilst Sir William went fishing with a reformed smuggler, Yawkins, Nelson and Emma explored the countryside in their carriage, visited country gentry and swam from a hired bathing machine.

Emma wrote several chatty letters from the comfort of her seafront hotel. 'We have got for dinner today a turtle dress'd and a haunch of venison – don't your mouth water?' she taunted Nelson's elder brother, William, a pompous parson. All the same she confessed, 'I should not like to be here in winter at all.'

When Emma returned to Merton to set up home for this strange *ménage à trois*, Nelson was desolate. He resented being left 'thumping in the Downs' and pronounced Deal 'the coldest place in England'.

A more cheerful guest was Sir Winston Churchill, Lord Warden of the Cinque Ports, who received the Freedom of Deal in 1951.

The Time Ball Tower

The Time Ball Tower was the earliest means of making Greenwich Mean Time known to shipping in the Downs. Its purpose was to signal accurate time – essential for mariners to determine their longtitude – to fleets passing through the English Channel.

During the Napoleonic Wars a line of overland shutter telegraph stations was established which, in fine weather, provided a system of rapid communication between the Admiralty in London and the Port Admiral at Deal. Signals were transmitted by means of pivoted shutters mounted on prominent buildings across Kent and this primitive device enabled coded messages to be conveyed by the Lords of the Admiralty at Whitehall to the Royal Navy fleet stationed in the Downs.

This revolutionary system was superceded by semaphore signalling invented by Rear Admiral Sir Home Riggs Popham. A purpose built Royal Signal Tower was constructed in 1820 at the entrance to the Navy Yard established at the beginning of the 18th century to provide light repairs, stores and provisions for Royal Navy warships in the Downs Anchorage.

This tower was intended as the terminus of a string of stations that would stretch across the county although this line was never completed. Instead, it was employed as the headquarters of the Coastal Blockade, formed to suppress smuggling on the coasts of Kent and Sussex.

In 1855, a time ball was positioned atop the redundant Semaphore Tower and this was linked by electric current following the line of the railway directly with the Royal Observatory at Greenwich. The ball, consisting of a hollow wooden sphere painted black, was mounted on a 14 ft square deal mast. It was dropped at 1 p.m. to signal the precise time for ship's masters to adjust their chronometers before setting off on a precarious sea voyage. Deal was therefore the first town in the world to receive Greenwich Mean Time.

First warden appointed was William Curling Newby and his fee (one guinea per week) included living accommodation in the tower, although an iron shaft descending through the upper storeys may have proved a trifle inconvenient. Last occupants were George Cutcher, a retired lieutenant, with his wife and children. On the day of the town's closure the whole family climbed to the top platform to have their photograph taken for posterity.

In 1927 the time ball was superceded by B.B.C. radio pips signals broadcast at specific times for the benefit of shipping and the G.P.O. speaking clock (TIM) Today, the replica ball is dropped hourly, purely as a tourist attraction, while the historic tower contains a museum devoted to time and telegraphy.

Old St. Mary's Church at Upper Walmer dates from circa 1120 and was probably built by Hugh d'Auberville, grandson of a valiant knight who was loyal to Duke William of Normandy. It was intended as a private chapel for the d'Aubervilles, the ruins of whose moated manor are still visible alongside the churchyard.

Originally, this typical Norman church consisted of a nave and chancel with north and south doorways. Its exterior is built of rough flint with ashlar stone dressings which indicates an early construction. Inside, a grand semi-circular chancel arch is embellished with rich carvings. A lofty Norman doorway with an equally impressive arch is concealed by a later porch. On the surrounding stones are traces of three medieval mass dials.

The interior of this little church contains numerous treasures. The font has an ancient stone bowl with a pyramidical deal cover dated '1664' on its carved knop. High on the north wall of the chancel hang the painted royal arms of George I. There are myriad monuments to distinguished naval families – most prominent of which are the Harveys.

The Duke of Wellington, Lord Warden of the Cinque Ports, was a punctilious attender of Old St. Mary's. Every Sunday when he was in residence at Walmer Castle he rode over to the church, a great Bible tucked under his arm, where he tied his horse to the ancient yew nearest the porch. Habitually, he would curl up in one corner of his private pew under the triple decker pulpit (since removed) and fall asleep during the long sermon, snoring loudly. The Duke expressed a wish to be buried in this humble village church. By custom, displaying his hatchment, armorial bearings, was carried ahead of his funeral procession. This lozenge shaped board, which shows only one of his innumerable 'achievements' – the Order of the Garter – hangs prominently in St Mary's.

The rambling churchyard contains several notable burials. Oldest tombstone lies opposite the south porch and recalls John Bassett (died 1680) a gunner from Walmer Castle. Later tombstones commemorate Elizabeth Norman (died 1842) the housekeeper at Walmer Castle and Duncan McArthur (died 1855) the physician who attended the Iron Duke. Nearby is the grave of John Kale (died 1840) from the 71st Regiment who bravely fought at Waterloo.

Over the centuries, Old St. Mary's was enlarged to accommodate an expanding congregation. Alas, the improvements were deemed unsympathetic and inadequate. In 1888, New St. Mary's was consecrated atop Constitution Hill as the magnificent parish church of Walmer.

Walmer Castle is the official residence of the Lord Warden of the Cinque Ports. Notable Lords Warden have included Prince George of Denmark, Queen Anne's consort; W.H. Smith, founder of the chain of stationers; Sir Winston Churchill, Britain's wartime Prime Minister, and Sir Robert Menzies, former Prime Minister of Australia.

Most illustrious was Sir Arthur Wellesley, Duke of Wellington, who resided here every autumn from his installation in 1829 until his death at the castle in 1852. A modest museum displays several relics of the Iron Duke, including his gruesome death mask and a pair of the celebrated Wellington boots.

The Iron Duke's study is furnished almost exactly as he knew it with his mahogany desk at which he stood to write and spartan camp bed that accompanied him on several campaigns. When Lady Salisbury asked how he found it possible to sleep in such a narrow bed his classic reply was: 'When it's time to turn over it's time to turn out!'

Queen Victoria and Prince Albert with their young family spent a holiday here in the autumn of 1842. The castle was greatly altered to make it more comfortable for the royal couple, whose presence attracted huge crowds of sightseers. The Queen enjoyed carriage rides around the town and excursions to Ramsgate and Dover. Prince Albert was rowed around the Downs and inspected the South Foreland lighthouse. An impromptu regatta was organised by local boatmen to celebrate the infant Princess Royal's birthday. Victoria and Albert relished their frequent walks, unrecognised, along the foreshore despite the wind and rain.

Walmer Castle's gardens are a delight. They were originally laid out by Lady Hester Stanhope, that eccentric neice of William Pitt. Britain's youngest Prime Minister was also Lord Warden during the Napoleonic Wars and referred to locally as: 'The Pilot that Weathered the Storm'.

The gardens were greatly admired by our most recent Lord Warden, H.M. Queen Elizabeth the Queen Mother. To celebrate Queen Elizabeth's 95th birthday a formal garden was created by Penelope Hobhouse to include favourite plants from Her Majesty's childhood homes. Today the castle's colourful gardens number a wild garden, a kitchen garden, a croquet lawn and the Broad Walk with its undulating yews and herbaceous borders.

The post of Lord Warden is a royal appointment although it is now regarded as an honorary one. Present Lord Warden is the former First Sea Lord, Admiral Lord Michael Boyce, who was installed on 12 April 2005. The ceremony at Dover Castle was marked by a flypast of Sea Harriers and a 19 gun salute from H.M.S. *Albion* in Dover Harbour.

Royal Marines – 'soldiers that serve at sea' – were formed early in the reign of Charles II. During the Civil War the proportion of seamen to soldiers had fallen considerably. At the Restoration of the Monarchy in 1660, an attempt was made to redress the balance by James, Duke of York and Albany (later James II) who was then Lord High Admiral.

His new regiment of sea-soldiers was known as 'The Duke of York and Albany's Regiment of Foote'. Unwisely, their uniform consisted of canary yellow which rendered them an easy target for snipers. (Yellow was the favourite colour of Prince James). In Victorian times their uniform was changed to khaki which proved a far more effective camouflage in battle.

Since their inception, Royal Marines have always had a close connection with the port although it was not until 1861 that a permanent base was established in barracks previously occupied by the army at Walmer.

And from the close of the French Wars until the First World War, Royal Marines

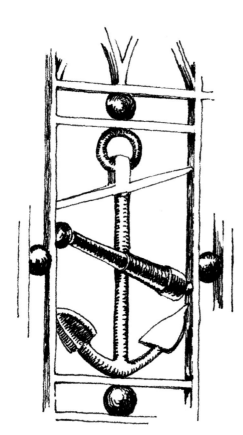

were rarely absent from active service, being engaged in the numerous minor battles that accompanied the expansion and consolidation of the British Empire. During the grand age of Imperialism in the 19th century, Royal Marines saw action in Burma, Mexico, Japan, Canada and New Zealand. They also participated in the Indian Mutiny, the three Chinese Wars, the Crimean War, the Zulu War and the Boer War.

Eventually, Royal Marines Deal Depot consisted of North, South (or 'Cavalry') and East Barracks. East Barracks remains a most imposing building – 365 feet long with a sequence of sash windows, a central pedimented portico and a cupola containing a clock – facing Walmer foreshore. It became the home of the world famous Royal Marines School of Music.

During World War Two, the Royal Marines Siege regiment manned two huge cross Channel guns – 'Winnie' and 'Pooh' – on the White Cliffs while 40 Commando trained at Deal before their epic raid on Dieppe in 1942. In recognition of their wartime service, the Freedom of Deal was conferred on the Royal Marines in 1945.

Deal and Walmer were justly proud of their long association with the Royal Marines. The celebrated band presented parades in summer, concerts in winter and traditionally led the carnival during the regatta. Sadly, following the detonation of a high explosive bomb by the I.R.A. in 1989, the Royal Marines were removed to Eastney, Portsmouth, in 1996. The extensive barracks were converted into luxury homes while a memorial bandstand still hosts open air concerts by visiting bands, including the Royal Marines, on Walmer Green.

Walmer Lifeboat exists to serve this perilous stretch of Kent coastline opposite the Goodwin Sands. A first lifeboat, *Royal Thames Yacht Club*, named after the society that presented her, was placed at Walmer in 1856. It was joined by North Deal lifeboat in 1865 and Kingsdown lifeboat in 1866.

These early rowing-sailing craft were manned by a coxswain and a voluntary crew formed from experienced local boatmen. Summoned by a bell, their crews comprised the first dozen men to arrive at the station and don oilskins, sou'westers and lifejackets.

All three lifeboats, launched from the open beach, worked in unison. Famous rescues number the sailing ship *Iron Crown* (1865), the steamship *Sorrento* (1872), the cargo ship *Helena Modjeska* (1947) and the French freighter *Agen* (1952).

A distinctive Lifeboat House on Walmer Green was specially built to hold the third lifeboat, *Centurion*, stationed there in 1871. Its ecclesiastical appearance deliberately mirrors St Saviour's Church, opposite.

First motor lifeboat, *Charles Dibdin Civil Service No. 2*, arrived at Walmer in 1933. It completely revolutionised lifesaving along this coast. The station now required a mechanic. This lifeboat frequently launched to assist vessels that had been mined or in collision in the blackout during World War Two. It was also involved in the evacuation of Dunkirk.

Throughout hostilities, Dr. James Hall OBE assumed the role of lifeboat doctor for allied shipping in the Downs. His exploits are related in his autobiography, *Sea Surgeon* (1960)

And in the immediate postwar period Walmer was the busiest lifeboat in the British Isles. During this traumatic time, there was an astonishing series of wrecks when American liberty ships – *Luray Victory*, *North Eastern Victory* – lacking competent pilots, foundered on the treacherous Goodwins. Walmer lifeboat also attended when the South Goodwin light vessel parted her riding cable and struck the Sands with loss of all hands in November 1954.

Last lifeboat was *Hampshire Rose* which entered service in 1975. A gift of the people of Hampshire (and Sussex) whose county emblem is a rose, she was launched by Lady Rose, wife of round-the-world lone yachtsman, Sir Alec Rose.

Today, owing to increased navigational aids, the role of the lifeboat service in Kent has changed. Emergency calls are now mainly to assist pleasure craft in difficulties immediately offshore. Walmer lifeboat now takes the form of an inflatable Atlantic 85 dingy, *Donald McLauchlan*, manned by a crew of five volunteers including a helmsman.

Three Piers have graced Deal seashore in times past whose fate and fortunes have mirrored the town's history.

Landing passengers and cargoes on the shingle beach in an open boat had always proved a risky business, particularly in rough weather. To solve this problem a short wooden pier was built immediately north of the Royal Hotel in 1838. The designer was Sir John Rennie, responsible for the construction of London Bridge. Each year the pier was battered by violent gales and weakened by sandworm. Finally, in 1857 a sudden storm brought the whole structure crashing down.

A second pleasure pier was constructed of wrought and cast iron in 1864. The designer was Eugenius Birch, the acclaimed builder of piers whose credits include Brighton and Blackpool. The thousand feet long structure had seating along its entire stem, was illuminated by globe lanterns and boasted a tramway for conveying luggage to waiting steamships. There were three decks – promenade, fishing and small boat – and at its seaward end was a cafe and concert hall. The Pier Master was a highly respected person who cut a jaunty figure in his nautical uniform.

Alas, this noble Victorian structure was constantly buffeted by stricken vessels in the Downs. Notable incidents involved the barque, *Merle*, in 1873 and the schooner, *Alliance*, in 1884. Finally, the Dutch motor vessel, *Nora*, carrying a cargo of straw boards was fatally struck by a sea mine in 1940. A heavy sea and rising tide carried her broadsides through the pier until she halted on the beach northwards. The remaining two thirds of the pier was blown up by the Royal Engineers on Churchill's orders because it obstructed the field of fire from coastal guns after the fall of France.

Deal's present pier was opened in 1957 by Prince Philip, Duke of Edinburgh. Built of reinforced concrete, with a thousand feet long stem leading to a modern cafe and lower fishing deck, it is the only pleasure pier to remain in Kent.

An invigorating stroll along this unique postwar pier is rewarded with a spectacular panorama of the coastline stretching from Kingsdown Cliffs southwards to an extensive view of Thanet in the north. On exceptionally fine days there are views over the Goodwin Sands and across the English Channel to France. And in between there is the enchanting townscape of Deal with its disorderly row of 18th and 19th century cottages, behind which peer the myriad spires and cupolas of churches and chapels.

Deal pier won the National Pier Society's 'Pier of the Year' award for 2008.

Archery Square is one of the most pleasant areas of Walmer. It takes its name from the formation of a popular Archery Club in mid Victorian times. Competitions regularly took place on the rectangular green bounded by mature trees leased from 'Park House'. Photographs show gentlemen in frock coats and top hats and ladies in crinolines and bonnets posing between the butts.

Sheltered 'Green Park' became Walmer Subscription Lawn Tennis and Croquet Ground. Established in 1883, it is one of the oldest lawn tennis clubs in the world. A flagstaff beyond the palings flies the club's colours (blue, red and white) while a sturdy timber clubhouse displays a collection of antique raquets.

Grand houses face each other across the enclosed lawn. Last to be built was the elegant terrace of six villas at the north-east corner completed in 1927. They were the inspiration of George Speaight, a master printer from London. Their construction practically bankrupted him. This delightful row, pristinely whitewashed, boasts sash windows with shutters, porches with overhead balconies, tall chimneys and attractive dormers which pierce the rippling pantiled roofs. A striking feature is the flamboyant end gable. The tiny walled front gardens are ablaze each summer with climbing roses and wisteria. At one time Nos. 38 and 40 were adjoined. The Prince of Wales (briefly Edward VIII) visited one summer while playing a round or two at the Royal Cinque Ports Golf Club. Prince Edward professed himself 'crazy keen' on the sport and subsequently hired a seaside cottage so that he could be close to the three links at Sandwich Bay.

Tucked away behind the square is a modest red brick building with high windows and a central doorway above which is the remnant of an ornate lantern. Formerly, this was a junior school partnered with the tiny infants school at the top of Drum Hill. Both schools were amalgamated to form The Downs Primary School. Further along Liverpool Road is a long terrace of former Coastguard cottages.

Grander dwellings are located on the east side. They each have an enclosed garden with Edwardian summerhouses bordering the sea. Although their main facades face seawards, the backs, painted in pleasing pastels, are equally impressive.

Joseph, Baron Lister, pioneer of antiseptic surgery, retired to No. 32 The Beach, known as 'The Coach House', in 1908. Lord Lister enjoyed carriage rides along the seafront and visits from younger relatives until he became an invalid. Then he contented himself with watching the spectacular sunsets from the intricate bow windows overlooking the tennis courts at the rear of his retirement home, also called 'Park House'.

Ripple Windmill is a conspicuous landmark across the fields of gaudy

yellow rape seed along the busy road from Upper Walmer to Dover. Ships in the English Channel found it such a recognisable feature that it was renovated by Trinity House in 1895.

Originally, this black wooden smock mill on its tall brick base was built at Drellingore, near Folkestone, at the close of the 18th century but transferred to its present site at the beginning of the 19th century. The method was to saw the eight corner posts – the 'cants' – down the centre and, when re-erecting, simpy bolt them together again. Unusually, there were three pairs of stones driven from underneath (as in a watermill) instead of from above, known as 'underdrift'.

Ripple Mill appears on a tithe map of 1840. At that time it was owned by Benjamin Horn and run by John Mummery. In those days, apparently, almost forty windmills could be viewed from the top of the octagonal tower with the aid of a telescope. A later visitor to the mill reported hearing the relentless thump of the engines of steamships as they rounded the South Foreland.

The Duke of Wellington habitually rode over the fields to hunt with his hounds while residing at Walmer Castle. The meet was at Ripple Mill and the Duke, who was a meticulous time keeper, invariably arrived ahead of the farmers who would start the fox. While waiting, he would tap on the door with his stick and call out in his thin sharp voice for Miller Mummery to come and chat. The unlikely pair would sit on the dusty sacks of bran inside the rumbling interior and discuss the horrors of war.

Finally, Ripple Mill was acquired by the Monins family. Captain John Monins was a cousin of Field Marshal Earl Kitchener, Secretary of War. Prior to the outbreak of the Great War, Lord Kitchener visited the mill and climbed to the summit to inspect the view over the Downs but while there a telegraph boy arrived to summon him to London. Later that day Miller Simpson found Kitchener's coat and reported it to Captain Monins. Kitchener sent word that the miller might keep the coat as he would not want it again. This proved to be a tragic prophecy since Lord Kitchener was drowned soon afterwards when his cruiser, H.M.S. *Hampshire*, taking him to Russia on a secret mission was torpedoed off Scapa Flow.

After the death of Captain John Monins in a motor car accident prior to the Second World War, Ripple Mill fell into disuse. In 1955, bereft of cap and sails, it was purchased by Rediffusion to support a television mast. Commendably, the present owners have restored it to perfection with its wooden machinery reconstructed from surviving plans turning the replica sails and fantail.

TOM BURNHAM is an admired artist whose charming watercolours are avidly collected. Brought up in Bath, Tom trained in graphic design at the renowned Bath Academy of Art. Later, his responsibilities as a manager for British Rail brought him into Kent where he was required to supervise the transport of materials for the construction of the Channel Tunnel. At that time, he and his family visited Deal and they fell in love with the place so much that they decided to settle there. Apart from recording the locality in the medium of watercolour, Tom is greatly involved in the local community. He is a stalwart member of Walmer Lawn Tennis Club and the Shotokan Karate Club. (He is a black belt!). He is also Secretary of the Deal and Walmer Inshore Fishermen's Association. Tom's wife, Marlene, was a former Town Mayor while their twin sons, Ben and Jack, are one of the few remaining commercial fishermen on Deal beach. Tom has been faithfully restoring a veteran pleasure boat, *Lady Irene*, now beached on the seafront adjacent to Deal Castle. This historic craft is probably one of the oldest, and certainly the most complete, beach boats in Britain. Tom is at present engaged in painting the windmills and watermills of Kent.

GREGORY HOLYOAKE is an actor, author and schoolteacher who lives in a flat overlooking the seafront at Deal. He trained as a schoolmaster at Culham College of Education, Oxfordshire, where he gained teaching diplomas in English Literature and Divinity. As an actor he trained at Rose Bruford College of Speech and Drama, Kent, before embarking on a theatrical career appearing in repertory and repertoire countrywide.

Gregory has been a photo-journalist for almost forty years and has appeared regularly in such national magazines as *Country Life, Country Homes and Interiors, This England, The Lady, Illustrated London News, Heritage* and *Evening Standard*. For five years he was chief reporter for *Kent Life* when he became an authority on Kent topics. He photographed *Kent - The County in Colour* for the Dovecote Press and *Scarecrows* for Unicorn Press. He has also written a trilogy of local histories – *Deal: Sad Smuggling Town, All in the Downs* and *Wellington At Walmer,* while his boyhood in postwar Kent is described in detail in *The Prefab Kid.* Gregory is currently researching the real Dick Whittington.